Alexander Hume: Of the Orthographie and Congruitie of the Britan Tongue

EARLY ENGLISH TEXT SOCIETY

Original Series, No. 5

1865 (second edition 1870;

reprinted 1965)

PRICE 12s. 6d.

Orthographie and Congruitie of the Britan Tongue

A Treates, noe shorter then necessarie

for the Schooles

Be

Alexander Hume

EDITED BY

HENRY B. WHEATLEY

Published for
THE EARLY ENGLISH TEXT SOCIETY
by the
OXFORD UNIVERSITY PRESS
LONDON   NEW YORK   TORONTO

OXFORD
UNIVERSITY PRESS

Great Clarendon Street, Oxford OX2 6DP
United Kingdom

Oxford University Press is a department of the University of Oxford.
It furthers the University's objective of excellence in research, scholarship,
and education by publishing worldwide. Oxford is a registered trade mark of
Oxford University Press in the UK and in certain other countries

© The Early English Text Society 1865

The moral rights of the authors have been asserted

Database right Oxford University Press (maker)

First Edition published in 1865
Second Edition 1870
Reprinted 1965

All rights reserved. No part of this publication may be reproduced,
stored in a retrieval system, or transmitted, in any form or by any means,
without the prior permission in writing of Oxford University Press,
or as expressly permitted by law, or under terms agreed with the appropriate
reprographics rights organization. Enquiries concerning reproduction
outside the scope of the above should be sent to the Rights Department,
Oxford University Press, at the address above

You must not circulate this book in any other form
and you must impose this same condition on any acquirer

Published in the United States of America by Oxford University Press
198 Madison Avenue, New York, NY 10016, United States of America

British Library Cataloguing in Publication Data
Data available

Library of Congress Cataloging in Publication Data
Data available

Original Series, 5

ISBN 978-0-19-722005-4

PREFACE.

THE following Tract is now printed for the first time from the original Manuscript in the old Royal Collection in the Library of the British Museum (Bibl. Reg. 17 A. xi). It is written on paper, and consists of forty-five leaves, the size of the pages being $5\frac{3}{4}$ in. by $3\frac{3}{4}$ in. The dedication, the titles, and the last two lines, are written with a different coloured ink from that employed in the body of the MS., and appear to be in a different handwriting.

The Manuscript is undated, and we have no means of ascertaining the exact time when it was written; but from a passage in the dedication to James I. of England, it is fair to infer that it was written shortly after the visit of that monarch to Scotland, subsequent to his accession to the throne of the southern kingdom, that is, in the year 1617. This would make it contemporaneous with Ben Jonson's researches on the English Grammar; for we find, in 1629, James Howell (Letters, Sec. V. 27) writing to Jonson that he had procured Davies' Welch Grammar for him, "to add to those many you have." The grammar that Jonson had prepared for the press was destroyed in the conflagration of his study; so that the posthumous work we now possess consists merely of materials, which were printed for the first time in 1640, three years after the author's death.

The Dedication of this Tract is merely signed *Alexander Hume*, and contains no other clue to the authorship. Curiously enough there were four Alexander Humes living about the same time, and three of them were educated at St Mary's College, St Andrew's; only two, however, became authors, the first of whom was Minister of Logie, and wrote *Hymnes or Sacred Songes*. There can be little doubt, however, that the present grammar was written by the Alexander Hume who was at one time Head Master of the High School, Edinburgh, and author of *Grammatica Nova*.

From Dr Steven's History of the High School, Edinburgh, and from M'Crie's Life of Melville, I have been enabled to extract and put together the following scanty particulars of our author's life :—The time and place both of his birth and of his death are alike unknown: but he himself, on the title of one of his works, tells us that he was distantly connected with the ancient and noble family of Home, in the county of Berwick. He was educated at the school of Dunbar, under the celebrated Andrew Simson, and in due time was enrolled a student in St Mary's College, St Andrew's, and then took the degree of Bachelor of Arts in 1574. He came to England, and was incorporated at Oxford, January 26, 1580-81, as "M. of A. of St Andrew's, in Scotland."[1] He spent sixteen years in England, partly engaged in studying and partly in teaching. During the latter part of this term he was a schoolmaster at Bath, as appears from Dr Hill's answer to him, published in 1592; and the fact of his residence in this city is corroborated at page 18 of the present treatise. He then returned to Scotland, having gained a reputation for the excellence of his learning and for the power he possessed of communicating it to others. On

[1] Wood's Fasti Oxonienses, by Bliss, i. 217.

the dismissal of Hercules Rollock, Rector of the High School, Edinburgh, from his office, Hume was unanimously chosen to succeed him, and his appointment was dated 23rd April, 1596. During his incumbency the High School underwent many changes, and received the form which it retains to the present day. In March, 1606, Hume resigned his office to become principal master in the grammar school founded a short time previously, at Prestonpans, by the munificent John Davidson, minister of the parish. The following document gives an account of Hume's admission to this school:—

"At hadintoun ye 25 of Junij 1606. The q^{lk} day M^r Jo^n ker minister of ye panis producit ye prēntat^{o}ne of Mr Alex^r hoome to be schoolm^r of ye schoole of ye panis foundit be Mr J^o Davedsone for instructioune of the youth in hebrew, greek and latine subscryvet be yais to quhome M^r Jo^n davedsone gave power to noiāt ye man q^{lk} prēntat^{o}ne ye prēbrie allowit and ordenit ye moderator & clerk to subscrive ye samine in y^r names q^{lk} yay ded. As also ordeanit y^t ye said kirk of ye panis suld be visited upon ye eight day of Julij next to come for admissione of ye said Mr Alex^r to ye said office. The visitors wer appoyntit M^r Ar^d oswald Mr Robert Wallace Mr George greir M^r andro blackhall & M^r andro Maghye to teach."——"At Saltprestoun July 8, 1606. The haill parischoners being poisit how yay lyckit of ye said Mr Alex^r w^t vniforme consent being particularly inqwyrit schew y^r guid lycking of him. and y^r willingnes to accept and receiv him to ye said office Q^{r}upon ye said Mr Alex^r wes admittit to ye said office & in token of ye approba^{o}ne both of visitors & of ye parischonēs p^{r}nt both ye ane and ye vother tuik ye said Mr Alex^r be ye hand & ye haill magistratis gentlemen and remanēt parischoners p^{r}nt faithfullie p^{r}misit to cōcurre for ye furtherāce of ye work y^t yit restis to be done to ye said schoole as also to keipt ye said Mr Alex^r and his scholleris skaithlis finallie for farther authorizing of ye said (*sic*) it wes thought meitt y^t ye haill visitors & parichonēs p^{r}nt suld enter ye said Mr Alex^r into ye said schoole & y^r heir him teache q^{lk} also wes doone." (Rec. of Presb. of Haddington).[1]

---

[1] M'Crie's Life of Melville, vol. ii., p. 509.

The school rapidly rose to distinction under Hume, but in 1615 he relinquished his position, and accepted the Mastership of the Grammar School of Dunbar, then in high repute, and the very same school in which he had commenced his own education. When occupied at Dunbar, Hume had the honour of being the first who, in a set speech, welcomed James VI. back to his Scottish dominions, after an absence of fourteen years. The King stopped on his way northward from Berwick on the 13th of May, 1617, at Dunglass Castle, the residence of the Earl of Home, and Hume, as the orator of the day, delivered a Latin address.

The date of Hume's death is not known; but he was witness to a deed on the 27th of November, 1627; and later still, in the records of the Privy Council of Scotland, 8th and 16th July, 1630, Mr D. Laing tells me that there is a memorandum of the King's letter anent the Grammar of Mr Alexander Hume, "schoolmaster at Dunbar." With regard to his private life, we know that he was married to Helen Rutherford, and had two sons and a daughter born to him in Edinburgh between the years 1601 and 1606. He was the father of three more children, also two sons and a daughter, between 1608 and 1610, in the county of East Lothian.

Hume was a master in controversy, and wrote on subjects of polemical divinity; but his mind was principally drawn towards language and the rules of its construction. He especially gave much of his time to the study of Latin grammar, and feeling dissatisfied with the elementary books which were then in use, he drew up one himself, which he submitted to the correction of Andrew Melville and other learned friends, and published in 1612 under the title of *Grammatica Nova*. The object he proposed to himself was to exclude from the schools the grammar of the Priscian of the Netherlands, the celebrated John Van Pauteren, but his work did not give the satisfaction which he had expected. He succeeded, however, in his wishes after many reverses, by the help of Alexander Seton, Earl of Dunfermline, Chancellor of Scotland, and by authority both of Parliament and of the Privy Council his grammar was enjoined to be used in all the schools of the kingdom. But through the interest of the bishops, and the steady opposition of Ray, his successor at the High School, the injunction was rendered of no effect. He would not, however, be beaten, and we find that in 1623 he was again actively engaged in adopting measures to secure the introduction of his grammar into every school in North Britain where the Latin language was taught.

The following is a list of our author's works :—

A Reioynder to Doctor Hil concerning the Descense of Christ into Hell. By Alexander Hume Maister of Artes. 4°.

No place of printing, printer's name, or date, but apparently printed at London in 1592 or 1593. Dedicated to Robert Earl of Essex. Although this is the first work that I can find attributed to Alexander Hume, yet there is no doubt that there must have been a former one of which we have no record, and the title and contents of Dr Hill's book would lead us to this conclusion—" The Defence of the Article : Christ descended into Hell. With arguments obiected against the truth of the same doctrine of one Alexander Humes. By Adam Hyll, D of Divinity. London 1592. 4°." This little volume consists of two parts ; 1st, the original sermon preached by Hill 28th February, 1589 ; 2nd, the reply to Hume. At p. 33, the end of the sermon, is this note, "This sermon . . . . . was answered by one Alexander Huns, Schoolemaester of Bath, whose answere wholy foloweth, with a replye of the author" . . . . At p. 33, " The reply of Adam Hill to the answere made by Alexander Humes to a sermon," etc.

A Diduction of the true and Catholik meaning of our Sauiour his words, *this is my bodie*, in the institution of his laste Supper through the ages of the Church from Christ to our owne dayis. Whereunto is annexed a Reply to M. William Reynolds in defence of M. Robert Bruce his arguments on this subject : displaying M. John Hammilton's ignorance and contradictions : with sundry absurdities following upon the Romane interpretation of these words. Compiled by Alexander Hume, Maister of the high Schoole of Edinburgh. Edinburgh, Printed by Robert Waldegrave, Printer to the King's Maiestie, 1602. Cum Privilegio Regis. 8°.

Prima Elementa Grammaticæ in usum juventutis Scoticæ digesta. Edinburgi, 1612. 8°.

Grammatica Nova in usum juventutis Scoticæ ad methodum revocata. Edinburgi, 1612. 8°.

Bellum Grammaticale, ad exemplar M^{ri} Alexandri Humii. Edinburgi, excud. Gideon Lithgo, Anno Dom. 1658 8°. Several later editions.

This humorous Grammatical Tragi-Comedy was not written by Hume, but only revised by him.

King James's Progresses, collected and Published by John Adamson afterwards Principal of the University of Edinburgh, entitled—

ΤΑ ΤΩΝ ΜΟΥΣΩΝ ΕΙΣΟΔΙΑ :

The Muses Welcome to the High and Mighty Prince James &^{c}. At his Majesties happie Returne to Scotland In Anno 1617. Edinburgh 1618, folio.

At page 1 : " His Majestie came from Bervik to Dunglas the xiij day of Maye, where was delivered this [latin] speach following by A. Hume."—At page 16, there are also a couple of Latin verses signed "Alexander Humius."

MS. in the British Museum. The present work.

MS. in the Advocates' Library :—

Rerum Scoticarum Compendium, in usum Scholarum. Per Alexandrum Humium ex antiqua et nobili gente Humiorum in Scotia, a primâ stirpe quinta sobole oriundum. This work is dated October 1660, and is therefore merely a transcript. It is an epitome of Buchanan's History, and Chr. Irvine in Histor. Scot. Nomenclatura, calls it Clavis in Buchananum, and Bishop Nicholson (Scottish Hist. Lib.) praises its Latin style.

The following three works are inserted by Dr Steven in his list of Hume's writings, and have been supposed to be his by M'Crie and others ; but, Mr D. Laing believes " there can be no doubt, from internal evidence, that the true author was Alexander Hume, the poet, who became minister of Logie, near Stirling, in 1597, and who died in December, 1609." In Wood's Athenæ Oxonienses, by Bliss, i. 624, it is stated that all three of them " were printed in London in 1594, in October," but this must, I think, be a mistake.

Ane Treatise of Conscience, quhairin divers secreits concerning that subject are discovered. At Edinburgh, printed by Robert Walde-grave, Printer to the King's Maiestie 1594. 8°.

Of the Felicitie of the world to come, unsavorie to the obstinate, alluring to such as are gone astray, and to the faithfull full of consolation. Edinb. 1594. 8".

Four Discourses, of Praises unto God, to wit, 1 in Praise of the Mercy and Goodness of God. 2 of his justice. 3 of his Power. 4 of his Providence. Edinb. 1594. 8°.

In conclusion, my acknowledgments are due to David Laing, Esq., who has kindly suggested some corrections in the list of Hume's works, in addition to what is noted above.

LONDON, FEBRUARY, 1865.

*To the maest excellent
in all princelie wis-
dom, learning, and he-
roical artes, JAMES,
of great Britan,
France, and
Ireland,
King,
Defender of the faeth,
grace, mercie, peace,
honoure here, and
glorie herafter.*

May it please your maest excellent M*ajestie*, I, your grace's humble servant, seeing sik uncertentie in our men's wryting, as if a man wald indyte one letter to tuentie of our best wryteres, nae tuae of the tuentie, without conference, wald agree; and that they quhae might perhapes agree, met rather be custom [fol. 1 b.] then knawlege, set my-selfe, about a yeer syne, to seek a remedie for that maladie. Quhen I had done, refyning it, I fand in Barret's alvearie,[1] quhilk is a dictionarie Anglico-latinum, that S*ir* Thomas Smith,[2] a man of nae less worth then learning, Secretarie to Queen Elizabeth, had left

---

[1] "An Alvearie or Quadruple Dictionarie, containing four sundrie tongues, namelie, English, Latine, Greeke and French .... by Jo. Baret. *London*, 1580." Folio. An edition was published in 1573, with three languages only, the Greek not being included.
[2] "De recta et emendata Linguæ Anglicæ Scriptione Dialogus. *Lutetiæ*, 1568." 4to.

DEDICATION.

a learned and judiciouse monument on the same subject. Heer consydering my aun weaknes, and meannes of my person, began to fear quhat might betyed my sillie boat in the same seas quhaer sik a man's ship was sunck in the gulf of oblivion. For the printeres and wryteres of this age, caring for noe more arte then may win the pennie, wil not paen them-selfes to knau whither it be orthographie or skaiographie that doeth the [fol 2.] turne : *and* schoolmasteres, quhae's sillie braine will reach no farther then the compas of their cap, content them-selfes with ἀυτὸς ἔφη my master said it. Quhil I thus hovered betueen hope *and* despare, the same Barret, in the letter E, myndes me of a star *and* constellation to calm al the tydes of these seaes, if it wald please the supreme Majestie to command the universitie to censure and ratifie, and the schooles to teach the future age right and wrang, if the present will not rectius sapere. Heere my harte laggared on the hope of your M*ajestie's* judgement, quhom God hath indeued with light in a sorte supernatural, if the way might be found to draue your eie, set on high materes [fol. 2 b.] of state, to take a glim of a thing of so mean contemplation, and yet necessarie. Quhiles I stack in this claye, it pleased God to bring your M*ajestie* hame to visit your aun Ida. Quher I hard that your G*race*, in the disputes of al purposes quherwith, after the exemple of *th*e wyse in former ages, you use to season your moat, ne quid tibi temporis sine fructu fluat, fel sundrie tymes on this subject reproving your courteoures, quha on a new conceat of finnes sum tymes spilt (as they cal it) the king's language. Quhilk thing it is reported that your M*ajestie* not onlie refuted with impregnable reasones, but alsoe fel on Barret's [fol. 3 a.] opinion that you wald cause the universities mak an Inglish gra*m*mar to repres the insolencies of sik green heades. This, quhen I hard it, soe secunded my hope, that in-continent I maed moien hou to convoy this litle treates to your M*ajestie's* sight, to further (if perhapes it may please your G*race*) that gud motion. In school materes, the least are not the least, because to erre in them is maest absurd. If the fundation be not sure, the maer gorgiouse the edifice the grosser the falt. Neither is it the least parte of a prince's praise, curasse rem literariam, and be his auctoritie to mend the [fol. 3 b.] misses that ignorant custom hath bred. Julius Cæsar was noe less diligent to eternize his name be the pen then be the suord. Neither thought he it unworthie of his paines to wryte a grammar in the heat of the civil weer, quhilk was to them as the English grammar is to us; *and*, as it seemes noe less then necessarie, nor our's is now. Manie kinges since that tyme have advanced letteres be erecting schooles, and doting revennues to their mantenance; but few have had the knaulege them-selfes to mend, or be tuiched with, the defectes or faltes crept into [fol. 4 a.] the boueles of learning, among quhom JAMES the first, ane of your M*ajestie's* worthie progenitoures, houbeit repressed be the iniquitie of the tyme, deserved noe smal praise; and your M*ajestie's* self noe less, commanding, at your first entrie to your Roial scepter, to reform the grammar, and to teach Aristotle in his aun tongue, quhilk hes maed the greek almaest as common in Scotland as the latine. In this alsoe, if it please your M*ajestie* to put to your hand, you have al the windes of favour [fol. 4 b.] in your sail; account, that al doe follow; judgement, that all doe reverence; wisdom, that al admire; learning, that stupified our scholes hearing a king borne, from tuelfe yeeres ald alwayes occupyed in materes of state, moderat in theological and philosophical disputationes, to the admiration of all that hard him, and speciallie them quha had spent al their dayes in those studies.

Accept, dred Soveragne, your pover servantes myte. If it can confer anie thing to the montan of your Majesties praise, and it wer but a clod, use it *and* the auctour as your's. [fol. 5 a.] Thus beseeking your grace to accep my mint, and pardon my miss, commites your grace to the king of grace, to grace your grace with al graces spiritual *and* temporal.

Your M*ajesties* hum-
ble servant,
Alexander Hume.

*OF THE ORTHOGRAPHIE
OF THE BRITAN TONGUE;
A TREATES, NOE
SHORTER
THEN NECESSARIE, FOR
THE SCHOOLES.*

[fol. 7 a.] OF THE GROUNDES OF ORTHOGRAPHIE.

CAP. 1.

1. To wryte orthographicallie ther are to be considered the symbol, the thing symbolized, and their congruence. Geve me leave, gentle reader, in a new art, to borrow termes incident to the purpose, quhilk, being defyned, wil further understanding.

2. The symbol, then, I cal the written letter, quhilk representes to the eie the sound that the mouth sould utter.

3. The thing symbolized I cal the sound quhilk the mouth utteres quhen the eie sees the symbol.

4. The congruence betuene them [fol. 7 b.] I cal the instrument of the mouth, quhilk, when the eie sees the symbol, utteres the sound.

5. This is the ground of al orthographie, leading the wryter from the sound to the symbol, and the reader from the symbol to the sound. As, for exemple, if I wer to wryte God, the tuich of the midle of the tongue on the roofe of the mouth befoer the voual, and the top of the tongue on the teeth behind the voual, myndes me to wryte it g o d. The voual is judged be the sound, as shal be shaued hereafter. This is the hardest lesson in this treates, and may be called the key of orthographie.

[fol. 8 a.] OF THE LATINE VOUALES.

CAP. 2.

1. We, as almaest al Europ, borrow our symboles from the Romanes. Quherforr, to rectefie our aun, first it behoves us to knaw their's. Thei are in number 23 : a, b, c, d, e, f, g, h, i, k, l, m, n, o, p, q, r, s, t, u, x, y, and z.

2. To omit the needles questiones of their order and formes ; of them, five be voualnes, ane a noat of aspiration, and all the rest consonantes.

3. A voual is the symbol of a sound maed without the tuiches of the mouth.

[fol. 8 b.] 4. They are distinguished the ane from the other be delating and contracting the mouth, and are a, e, i, o, u.

5. Quhat was the right roman sound of them is hard to judge,

seeing now we heer nae romanes; and other nationes sound them after their aun idiomes, and the latine as they sound them.

6. But seeing our earand is with our aun britan, we purpose to omit curiosities, *et* quæ nihil nostra intersunt. Our aun, hou-beit dialectes of ane tong, differing in the sound of them, differ alsoe in pronuncing the latine. Quherfoer, to make a conformitie baeth in latine and English, we man begin with the latine.

[fol. 9 a.] 7. A, the first of them, the south soundes as beath thei and we sound it in bare, nudus; and we, as beath thei and we sound it in bar, obex.

8. But without partialitie (for in this earand I have set my compas to the loadstar of reason), we pronunce it better. If I am heer deceaved, reason sall deceave me.

9. For we geve it alwaies ane sound beath befoer and behind the consonant: thei heer ane and ther an other. As in amabant, in the first tuae syllabes they sound it as it soundes in bare,.and in the last as it soundes in bar. Quherupon I ground this argument. That is the better sound, not onelie of this, but alsoe of al other letteres, q*uhi*lk is alwayes ane. But we sound it alwayes ane, and therfoer better.

[fol. 9 b.] Ad that their sound of it is not far unlyke the sheepes bae, q*uhi*lk the greek symbolizes be η not α, βη not βα. See Eustat. in Homer.

10. Of this letter the latines them-selfes had tuae other sounds differing the ane from the other, and beath from this, quhilk they symbolized be adding an-other voual, æ and au. And these they called diphthonges.

11. The diphthong they defyne to be the sound of tuae vouales coalescing into ane sound, quhilk definition in au is plaen, in æ obscurer as now we pronunce it, for now we sound it generallie lyke the voual e, without sound of the a, q*uhi*lk, notwithstanding is the principal voual in this diphthong sound. Questionles at the first it semes to have had sum differing sound from a, sik as we pronunce in stean, or the south in stain. But this corruption is caryed with a stronger tyde then reason can resist, and we wil not [fol. 10 a.] strive with the stream.

14. E followes, q*uhi*lk in reason sould have but ane sound, for

without doubt the first intent was to geve everie sound the awn symbol, and everie symbol the awn sound. But as now we sound it in quies and quiesco, the judiciouse ear may discern tuae soundes. But because heer we differ not, I wil acquiess. My purpose is not to deal with impossibilities, nor to mend al crookes, but to conform (if reason wil conform us) the south and north beath in latine and in English.

15. Af this voual ryseth tuae diphthonges, ei and eu, quhilk beath standes wel with the definition, sect. 11.

16. Of the next, i, we differ farder, and the knot harder to louse, for nether syde wantes [fol. 10 b.] sum reason. Thei in mihi, tibi, and sik otheres, pronunce it as it soundes in bide, manere; we as it soundes in bid, jubere.

17. Among the ancientes I fynd sum groundes for their sound. Cic. epist. fam. lib. 9, epis. 22, avoues that bini, in latin, and βίνει, in greek, had ane sound. And Varro, with sundrie ancientes, wrytes domineis and serveis, for dominis and servis, quhilk is more lyke the sound of bide then bid. If this argument reached as wel to i short as i lang, and if we wer sure how ει was pronunced in those dayes, this auctoritie wald over-weegh our reason; but seing i, in mihi, *etc.*, in the first is short, and in the last common, and the sound of ei uncertan, I stand at my reason, sect. 9, quhilk is as powerful heer for i as ther for a. They [fol. 11 a.] pronunce not i in is and quis, id and quid, in and quin, as they pronunce it in mihi, tibi, sibi, ibi, *etc.*, and therfoer not right.

18. As for o, in latin, we differ not; u, the south pronunces quhen the syllab beginnes or endes at it, as eu, teu for tu, and eunum meunus for unum munus, quhilk, because it is a diphthong sound, and because they them-selfes, quhen a consonant followes it, pronunce it other wayes, I hoep I sal not need argumentes to prove it wrang, and not be a pure voual.

OF THE BRITAN VOUALES.
Cap. 3.

1. Of a, in our tongue we have four soundes, al so differing [fol. 11 b.] ane from an-other, that they distinguish the verie signification of wordes, as, a tal man, a gud tal, a horse tal.

2. Quherfoer in this case I wald commend to our men the imitation of the greek and latin, quho, to mend this crook, devysed diphthonges. Let the simplest of these four soundes, or that quhilk is now in use, stand with the voual, and supplie the rest with diphthonges; as, for exemple, I wald wryte the king's hal with the voual a; a shour of hael, with ae; hail marie, with ai; and a heal head, as we cal it, quhilk as the English cales a whole head, with ea. And so, besydes the voual, we have of this thre diphthonges, tuae with a befoer, ae and ai, and ane with the e befoer, ea. Ad to them au, howbeit of a distinct sound; as, knaulege with us, in the [fol. 12 a.] south knowlege.

3. These and al other diphthonges I wald counsel the teacheres not to name be the voules quherof they are maed, but be the sound quhilk they maek, for learneres wil far maer easelie take the sound from the mouth of the teacher, then maek it them-selves of the voules ingredient.

4. Of e, we have tuae soundes, quhilk it is hard to judge quhilk is simplest; as, an el, ulna; and an el, anguilla; hel, infernus; and an hel, calx pedis. Heer I wald commend to our men quhae confoundes these the imitation of the south, quhilk doth wel distinguish these soundes, wryting the el, ulna, with the [fol. 12 b.] voual e, and eel, anguilla, with the diphthong ee. I am not ignorant that sum symbolizes this sound with a diphthong maed of ie; eie, oculus; hiel, fiel, miel, etc. Here I am indifferent, and onelie wishes that the ane be used; let the advysed judge make choise of quhilk, for my awne paert I lyke the last best; 1. becaus eie, oculus, can not wel be symbolized ee; 2. because the greekes expresse η be εε, quhilk, as appeares be the Ioneanes and doreanes, drawes neerar to α then ε.

5. Of i, also, our idiom receaves tuae soundes, as in a man's wil, and the wil of a fox. Heer, also, I wald have our men learne of the south, for these soundes they wel distinguish, wryting wil, fil, mil, stil, with i; and wyl, fyl, myl, styl, with y.

[fol. 13 a.] 6. Heer I see be Barrat, in his Alvearie, that sum wald be at symbolizing these soundes, the ane with the greek diphthong ει, and the other with ι inverted; as, rɩɩd equitare; bɛɩd, manere; rɩd, legere; hɩd, cavere. In this opinion I se an ege of judgement, and therfoer wil not censure it, except I saw the auctour's whole[1] drift. Onelie for my awn parte I will avoid al novelties, and content my self with the letteres q*uhi*lk we have in use. And seeing we have no other use of y distinguished from i, I condiscend to the opinion of the south using i for the ane, and y for the other.

7. O, we sound al alyk. But [fol. 13 b.] of it we have sundrie diphthonges: oa, as to roar, a boar, a boat, a coat; oi, as coin, join, foil, soil; oo, as food, good, blood; ou, as house, mouse, *etc*. Thus, we commonlie wryt mountan, fountan, q*uhi*lk it wer more etymological to wryt montan, fontan, according to the original.

8. In this diphthong we co*m*mit a grosse errour, saving better judgement, spelling how, now, and siklyk with w, for if w be (as it sal appear, quhen we cum to the awn place of it) a consonant, it can noe wayes coälesse into a diphthong sound, sik as this out of controversie is.

9. U, the last of this rank, the south, as I have said in the latin sound of it, pronu*n*ces eu, we ou, both, in my simple judgement, wrang, for these [fol. 14 a.] be diphthong soundes, and the sound of a voual sould be simple. If I sould judge, the frensh sound is neerest the voual sound as we pronu*n*ce it in mule and muse.

10. Of it we have a diphthong not yet, to my knawlege, observed of anie; and, for my awn parte, I am not wel resolved neither how to spel it, nor name it. Onelie I see it in this, to bou, a bow. I wait not quhither I sould spel the first buu, or the last boau. As, for exemple, if Roben hud wer nou leving, he wer not able to buu his aun bou, or to bou his aun boau. And therfoer this with al the rest, hou be it in other I have more for me, I leave to the censure of better judgement.

[fol. 14 b.]   OF CONSONANTES.

CAP. 4.

1. This for the vouales, and diphthonges maed of them without the tuiches of the mouth. Now followe the consonantes.

2. A consonant is a letter symbolizing a sound articulat that is broaken with the tuiches of the mouth.

---

[1] *hael* struck through and *whole* written above it.

3. The instrumentes of the mouth, quherbe the vocal soundes be broaken, be in number seven. The nether lip, the upper lip, the outward teeth, the inward teeth, the top of the tongue, the midle tong, and roof of the mouth. Of these, thre be, as it wer, hammeres stryking, and the rest stiddies, kepping the strakes of the hammeres.

4. The hammeres are the nether [fol. 15 a.] lip, the top of the tongue, and the midle tongue. The stiddies the overlip, the outward teeth, the inward teeth, and the roofe of the mouth.

5. The nether lip stryking on the overlip makes b, m, p, and on the teeth it makes f and v.

6. The top of the tongue stryking on the inward teeth formes d, l, n, r, s, t, and z.

7. The midle tongue stryking on the rouf of the mouth formes the rest, c, g, k, j, q, and x, and so we have 18 consonantes borrowed of the latines.

8. These they borrow al from the greekes, saving j and v, quhilk our age soundes other wayes then it seemes the romanes [fol. 15 b.] did; for Plutarch, more then 100 yeeres after Christ, expressing the sound quhilk they had in his tyme, symbolizes them neerar the sound of the vouales quherof they are maed then now we sound them in latin, for in Galba he symbolizes junius vindex, ιόυνιος όυινδεξ, quhilk, if then it had sounded as now we sound it, he sould rather have written it with γ and β, γόυνιος βίνδεξ.

9. We have in our use the sam soundes quhilk it seemes these consonantes had in plutarch's dayes, as in yallou, winter. Quhilk, seeing now they are worn out of the latin use, my counsel is that we leave the sound of them quhilk now is in the latin use to the [fol. 16 a.] latines, and take as our's the sound quhilk they have left, and geve to the sound, quhilk now we use in latin, the latin symbol; as, jolie jhon; vertue is not vain; and to the soundes quhilk they have left the symboles quhilk we have usurped to that end; as, yallou, youk; water, wyne.

10. And heer, to put our men af their errour quho had wont to symboliz yallou with an z, and to put noe difference betueen v and w, z is a dental consonant, broaken betueen the top of the tongue and root of the teeth; yal, a guttural sound, made be a mynt of the midle

tongue to the roofe of the mouth, and therfoer the organes being [fol. 16 b.] so far distant, and the tuich so diverse, this symbol can be no reason serve that sound, nor nane of that kynd.

11. As for v and w, seeing we have in our idiom, besyd the latin sound, an other never hard in latin, as now it is pronu*n*ced, I can not but co*m*mend the wisdom of the south, q*uh*ilk gave the latin sound their awn symbol, and took to our sound a symbol quhilk they use not. Lyke was their wisdom in j and y; for as the latines usurped the voual i for a consonant in their use, q*uh*ilk the greekes had not, so they usurped y, a voual not mikle different from i, for the correspondent sound, not used in the latin as now it is pronu*n*ced.

12. Heerfoer, for distinctiones of both sound and symbol, I wald [fol. 17 a.] commend the symbol and name of i and u to the voual sound; as, indifferent, unthankful; the symboles of j and v to the latin consonantes, and their names to be jod and vau; as, vain jestes; and the symboles y and w to our English soundes, and their names to be ye and we, or yod and wau; as, yonder wel, yallou wool.

13. Now remaineth h, q*uh*ilk we have called a noat of aspiration, cap. 2, sect. 2, and is, in deed, noe voual, because with a consonant it makes noe sound; as, ch; nor consonant, because it is pronu*n*ced without the tuich of the mouth; as, ha.

14. It may affect al voules *and* diphthonges; as, hand, hen, hind, hose, hurt, hail, hautie, health, heel, heifer, *etc.* But behind [fol. 17 b.] the voual in our tong (so far as yet I can fynd) it hath no use. Of consonantes, it affecteth g beyond the voual; as, laugh; p befoer the voual; as, phason; s and t also befoer the voual; as, think, shame. With c we spil the aspiration, turni*ng* it into an Italian chirt; as, charitie, cherrie, of quhilk hereafter.

OF OUR ABUSING SUM CONSONANTES.

Cap. 5.

1. Now I am cum to a knot that I have noe wedg to cleave, and wald be glaed if I cold hoep for help. Ther sould be for everie sound that can occur one symbol, and of everie symbol but one onlie

sound. This reason and nature craveth; and I can not but trow but that the worthie inventoures of this divyne facultie shot at this mark.

[fol. 18 a.] 2. But, contrarie to this sure ground, I waet not be quhat corruption, we see, not onelie in our idiom, but in the latin alsoe, one symbol to have sundrie soundes, ye, and that in one word; as, lego, legis.

3. First, to begin with c, it appeeres be the greekes, quho ever had occasion to use anie latin word, quharein now we sound c as s, in their tymes it sounded k; for Cicero, thei wryt kikero; for Cæsar, kaisar; and plut., in Galba, symbolizes principia, πρινκίπια.

4. This sound of it we, as the latines, also keepe befoer a, o, and u; as, canker, conduit, cumber. But, befoer e and i, sum tymes we sound it, with the latin, lyke an s; as, cellar, certan, cease, citie, circle, etc.

[fol. 18 b.] 5. Behind the voual, if a consonant kep it, we sound it alwayes as a k; as, occur, accuse, succumb, acquyre. If it end the syllab, we ad e, and sound it as an s; as, peace, vice, solace, temperance; but nether for the idle e, nor the sound of the s, have we anie reason; nether daer I, with al the oares of reason, row against so strang a tyde. I hald it better to erre with al, then to stryve with al and mend none.

6. This consonant, evin quher in the original it hes the awne sound, we turn into the chirt we spak of, cap. 4, sect. 14, quhilk, indeed, can be symbolized with none, neither greek nor latin letteres; as, from cano, chant; from canon, chanon; from castus, chast; from κυριακή, a [fol. 19 a.] church, Of quhilk I hard doctour laurence, the greek professour in Oxfoord, a man bothe of great learning and judgement, utter his opinion to this sense, and (excep my memorie fael me) in these wordes: κυριακὴ ut βασιλικὴ suppresso substantivo ὀικία domus domini est. Unde nostrum derivatur, quod Scoti et Angli boreales recte, pronunciant a kyrk, nos corrupte a church.

7. Yet, notwithstanding that it is barbarouse, seing it is more usual in our tongue then can be mended befoer the voual, as chance, and behind the voual, as such, let it be symbolized, as it is symbolized with ch, hou beit nether the [fol. 19 b.] c nor the h hath anie affinitie with that sound; 1, because it hath bene lang soe used; and 2,

because we have no other mean to symbolize it, except it wer with a new symbol, qu*h*lk it will be hard to bring in use.

8. Now, quheras ch in nature is c asperat, as it soundes in charus and chorus; and seing we have that sound also in use, as licht, micht; if I had bene at the first counsel, my vote wald have bene to have geven ch the awn sound. But as now the case standes, ne quid novandum sit, quod non sit necesse, I not onlie consent, but also commend the wisdom of the south, quho, for distinction, wrytes light, might, with gh, and referres ch to the other sound, how be it improperlie, and this distinction I commend [fol. 20 a.] to[1] our men, quho yet hes not satis attente observed it.

9. Next cumes g, how be it not so deformed as c; for, althogh we see it evin in latin, and that, in one word (as is said cap. 5, sect. 2), distorted to tuo soundes, yet both may stand with the nature of the symbol and differ not in the instrumentes of the mouth, but in the form of the tuich, as the judiciouse ear may mark in ago, agis; agam, ages.

10. This consonant, in latin, never followes the voual; befoer a, o, u, it keepes alwayes the awn sound, and befoer e and i breakes it.

11. But with us it may both begin and end the syllab; as, gang; it may, both behind and befoer, [fol. 20 b.] have either sound; as, get, gist, gin, giant.

12. These the south hath providentlie minted to distinguish tuo wayes, but hes in deed distinguished noe way, for the first sum hath used tuo gg; as, egg, legg, bigg, bagg; for the other dg; as, hedge, edge, bridge; but these ar not κατὰ πάντος. Gyles, nomen viri, can not be written dgiles; nor giles doli, ggiles; nether behind the voual ar they general; age, rage, suage, are never wrytten with dg. Quherfoer I conclud that, seeing nether the sound nor the symbol hath anie reason to be sundrie, without greater auctoritie, nor the reach of a privat wit, this falt is incorrigible.

13. Here I am not ignorant quhat a doe the learned make about the symboles of c, g, k and q, that they be al symboles, but of one sound; [fol. 21 a.] but I wil not medle in that question, being besyde my purpose, qu*h*lk is not to correct the latin symboles, but to fynd the best use of them in our idiom.

[1] MS. to to.

14. T, the last of these misused souldioures, keepes alwayes it's aun nature, excep it be befoer tio; as, oration, declamation, narration; for we pronunce not tia and tiu as it is in latin. Onelie let it be heer observed that if an s preceed tio, the t keepes the awn nature, as in question, suggestion, *etc.*

15. Thus have I breeflie handled the letteres and their soundes, quhilk, to end this parte, I wald wish the printeres, in their a, b, c, to expresse thus :—a, ae, ai, au, ea, b, c, d, e, ee, ei, eu, f, g, h, i, j, k, l, m, n, o, oa, oo, ou, p, q, r, s, t, u, ui, v, w, x, y, z, [fol. 21 b.] and the masteres teaching their puples to sound the diphthonges, not be the vouales quherof they be made, but be the sound quhilk they mak in speaking; lyk-wayes I wald have them name w, not duble u nor v, singl u, as now they doe; but the last, vau or ve, and the first, wau or we; and j, for difference of the voual i, written with a long tail, I wald wish to be called jod or je.

OF THE SYLLAB.
Cap. 6.

1. Now followes the syllab, quhilk is a ful sound symbolized with convenient letteres, and consistes of ane or moe.

2. A syllab of ane letter is symbolized with a voual onelie; as, a in able, e in ever, i in idle, o in over, u in unitie, for a consonant can make no syllab alane.

3. A syllab of moe letteres is made of vouales onelie, or els of vouales and consonantes. Of onlie vouales [fol. 22 a.] the syllab is called a diphthong, of quhilk we have spoaken in the vouales quherof they ar composed.

4. A syllab of vouales and consonantes either beginnes at the voual, as al, il, el; or at one consonant, as tal man; or at tuo consonantes, as stand, sleep; or els at thre at the maest, as strand, stryp. It endes either at a voual, as fa, fo; or at one consonant, as ar, er; or at tuo, as best, dart; or at thre at the maest, as durst, worst.

5. Heer is to be noated, that in divyding syllabes, the consonantes, one or moe, that may begin a syllab anie way in the middes of a word belong to the voual following, as in que-stion, qua-rel, fi-shar, sa-fron, ba-stard, de-scrib, re-scue.

[fol. 22 b.] 6. It is alsoe heer to be observed in printing and wryting, that quhen a word fales to be divyded at the end of a lyne, that the partition must be made at the end of a syllab, soe that the one lyne end at the end of the whol syllab, and the other begin the next lyne. As, for exemple, if this word magistrat fel to be divided at the first syllab, it behoved to be ma-gistrat; if at the second, it behoved to be magi-strat; but no wayes to parte the m from the a, nor the g from the i, nor the s from t, nor the t from r.

OF THE RULES TO SYMBOLIZE.
CAP. 7.

1. To symboliz right, the sound of the voual is first to be observed, quhither it be a simple voual or a [fol. 23 a.] compound, and quhilk of them is to be chosen, for quhilk no rule can be geven but the judgement of the ear.

2. Next the consonantes are to be marked; and first, quhither they break the voual befoer or behind; then quhither they be one or moe; and lastlie, with quhat organes of the mouth they be broaken.

3. For be the organes of the mouth, quherwith the syllab is broaken, the consonantes are discerned be quhilk the syllab must be symbolized, quhilk we have said, cap 1, sect. 5.

4. The consonantes may differ in hammar (as we called it, cap. 4, sect. 3) and stiddie, as b and d. Or they may agre in hammer and differ in stiddie, as b and v. Or they [fol. 23 b.] may agre in both and differ in the tuich, as f and v, m and p, c and g.

5. The tuich befoer the voual is be lifting the hammer af the stiddie; as da, la, pa; and behind, be stryking the hammer on the stiddie; as ad, al, ap. And quhen the hammer and the stiddie are ane, the difference is in the hardnes and softnes of the tuich; as may be seen in ca and ga, ta and da. But w and y maekes sae soft a mynt that it is hard to perceave, and therfoer did the latines symboliz them with the symbol of the voualles. They are never used but befoer the voual; as we, ye, wil, you; behynd the voual thei make noe consonant sound, nor sould be written, and therfore now and vow, with sik otheres, are not [to] be written with w, as is said befoer.

[fol. 24 a.] 6. Of this quhilk now is said may be gathered that general, quhilk I called the keie of orthographie, cap. 1, sect. 5, that is the congruence of the symbol and sound symbolized; that is, that bathe must belang to the same organes and be tuiched after the same form.

7. And, be the contrarie, here it is clere that soundes pronunced with this organ can not be written with symboles of that; as, for exemple, a labiel symbol can not serve a dental nor a guttural sound; nor a guttural symbol a dental nor a labiel sound.

8. To clere this point, and alsoe to reform an errour bred in the south, and now usurped be our ignorant printeres, I wil tel quhat befel my-self [fol. 24 b.] quhen I was in the south with a special gud frende of myne. Ther rease, upon sum accident, quhither quho, quhen, quhat, *etc.*, sould be symbolized with q or w, a hoat disputation betuene him and me. After manie conflictes (for we oft encountered), we met be chance, in the citie of baeth, with a doctour of divinitie of both our acquentance. He invited us to denner. At table my antagonist, to bring the question on foot amangs his awn condisciples, began that I was becum an heretik, and the doctour spering how, ansuered that I denyed quho to be spelled with a w, but with qu. Be quhat reason? quod the *Doctour*. Here, I beginning to lay my grundes of labial, dental, and guttural soundes and symboles, he snapped me on this hand and he [fol. 25 a.] on that, that the *doctour* had mikle a doe to win me room for a syllogisme. Then (said I) a labial letter can not symboliz a guttural syllab. But w is a labial letter, quho a guttural sound. And therfoer w can not symboliz quho, nor noe syllab of that nature. Here the *doctour* staying them again (for al barked at ones), the proposition, said he, I understand; the assumption is Scottish, and the conclusion false. Quherat al laughed, as if I had bene dryven from al replye, and I fretted to see a frivolouse jest goe for a solid ansuer. My proposition is grounded on the 7 sectio of this same cap., quhilk noe man, I [fol. 25 b.] trow, can denye that ever suked the paepes of reason. And soe the question must rest on the assumption quhither w be a labial letter and quho a guttural syllab. As for w, let the exemples of wil, wel, wyne, juge quhilk are sounded befoer the voual with a mint of

the lippes, as is said the same cap., sect. 5. As for quho, besydes that it differres from quo onelie be aspiration, and that w, being noe perfect consonant, can not be aspirated, I appele to al judiciouse eares, to qu*h*ilk Cicero attributed mikle, quhither the aspiration in quho be not ex imo gutture, and therfoer not labial.

OF RULES FROM THE LATIN.
Cap. 7 (*sic*).

1. Heer, seeing we borrow mikle from the latin, it is reason that [fol. 26 a.] we either follow them in symbolizing their's, or deduce from them the groundes of our orthographie.

2. Imprimis, then, quhatever we derive from them written with c we sould alsoe wryte with c, howbeit it sound as an s to the ignorant; As conceave, receave, perceave, from concipio, recipio, percipio; Concern, discern, from concerno, discerno; accesse, successe, recesse, from accedo, succedo, recedo, with manie moe, qu*h*ilk I commend to the attention of the wryter.

3. Also quhat they wryte w*i*th s we sould alsoe wryte with s; As servant, from servus; sense, from sensus; session from sessio; passion, from passio.

4. Neither is the c joined w*i*th s here to be omitted; As [fol. 26 b.] science and conscience, from scientia, conscientia; ascend and descend, from ascendo, descendo; rescind *and* abscind, from rescindo *and* abscindo.

4 (*sic*). This difference of c and s is the more attentivelie to be marked for that wordes of one sound and diverse signification are many tymes distinguished be these symboles; As, the kinges secrete council, and the faithful counsil of a frende; concent in musik, and consent of myndes; to duel in a cel, and to sel a horse; a décent weed, and descént of a noble house. These tuo last differres alsoe in accent.

5. Lykwayes, that we derive from latin verbales in tio, sould also be wrytten with t; as oration, visitation, education, vocation, proclamation, admonition, *etc.*

6. Wordes deryved from the [fol. 27 a.] latin in tia and tium we wryte with ce; as justice, from justitia; Intelligence, from intel-

ligentia; vice, from vitium; service, from servitium. In al qu*h*ilk, houbeit the e behind the c be idle, yet use hes made it tollerable to noat the breaking of the c, for al tongues bear with sum slippes that can not abyde the tuich stone of true orthographie.

7. C is alsoe written in our wordes deryved from x in latin; As peace, from pax; fornace, from fornax; matrice, from matrix; nurice, from nutrix, qu*h*ilk the south calles nurse, not without a falt both in sound and symbol; be this we wryte felicitie, audacitie, tenacitie, *etc.*

8. Lykwayes we sould keep the vouales of the original, quherin the north warres the [fol. 27 *b.*] south; from retineo, the north retine, the south retain; from foras, the north foran, the south forain; from regnu*m*, the north regne, the south raigne; from cor, the north corage, the south courage; from devoro, the north devore, the south devour; from vox, the north voce, the south voice; from devoveo, the north devote, the south devoute; from guerrum, the north were, the south war; from gigas, gigantis, the north gyant, the south giaunt; from mons, montis, the north mont, the south mount. Of this I cold reckon armies, but wil not presume to judge farther then the compass of my awn cap, for howbeit we keep nearar the original, yet al tongues have their idiom in borrowing from the latin, or other foran tongues.

OF SUM IDIOMES IN OUR ORTHOGRAPHIE.
Cap. 8.

[fol. 28 *a.*] 1. In our tongue we have sum particles qu*h*ilk can not be symbolized with roman symboles, nor rightlie pronunced but be our awn, for we in manye places soe absorb l and n behynd a consonant, quher they can not move without a voual intervening, that the ear can hardlie judge quhither their intervenes a voual or noe.

2. In this case sum, to avoid the pronu*n*ciation of the voual befoer the l and n, wrytes it behind; as litle, mikle, muttne, eatne. Quhilk houbeit it incurres in an-other inconvenience of pronu*n*cing the voual behind the l or n, yet I dar not presume to reprove, [fol. 28 *b.*] because it passeth my wit how to avoid both inconveniences, And therfoer this I leave to the wil of the wryter.

3. Sum of our men hes taken up sum unusual formes of sym-

bolizing, qu*h*ilk I wald wish to be reformed, yet If I bring not reason, let noe man change for my phantasie.

4. First, for peple they wryte people, I trow because it cumes from populus; but if that be a reason, I wald understand a reason quhy they speak not soe alsoe. Or gif they speak not soe, I wald understand quhy they wryte not as they speak. I knawe they have the exemple of france to speak ane way and wryte an-other; but that exemple[1] is as gud to absorb the s in the end of everie word. Al exemples are not imitable.

[fol. 29 *a.*] 5. They use alsoe to wryte logicque, musicque, rhetoricque, and other of that sorte, with cque. If this be doon to make the c in logica, *etc.*, subsist, quhy wer it not better to supply a k in the place of it, then to hedge it in with a whol idle syllab; it wer both more orthographical and easier for the learner, for c and k are sa sib, *that* the ane is a greek and the other a latin symbol of one sound. In this art it is alyke absurd to wryte that thou reades not, as to read that thou wrytes not.

6. We use alsoe, almost at the end of everie word, to wryte an idle e. This sum defend [fol. 29 *b.*] not to be idle, because it affectes the voual before the consonant, the sound quherof many tymes alteres the signification; as, hop is altero tantum pede saltare, hope is sperare; fir, abies, fyre, ignis; a fin, pinna, fine, probatus; bid, jubere, bide, manere; with many moe. It is true that the sound of the voual befoer the consonant many tymes doth change the signification; But it is as untrue that the voual e behind the consonant doth change the sound of the voual before it. A voual devyded from a voual be a consonant can be noe possible meanes return thorough the consonant into the former voual. Consonantes betuene vouales are lyke partition walles betuen roomes. Nothing can change the sound of a voual [fol. 30 *a.*] but an-other voual coalescing with it into one sound, Of qu*h*ilk we have spoken sufficientlie, cap. 3, to illustrat this be the same exemples, saltare is to hop; sperare to hoep; abies is fir; ignis, fyr, or, if you wil, fier; jubere is bid; manere, byd or bied.

7. Yet in sum case we ar forced to tolerat this idle e; 1. in wordes ending in c, to break the sound of it; as peace, face, lace,

---

[1] MS. exenple.

justice, *etc.* ; 2. behind s, in wordes wryten with this s ; as false, ise, case, muse, use, *etc.* ; 3. behind a broaken g; as knawlege, savage, suage, ald age. Ther may be moe, and these I yeld because I ken noe other waye to help this necessitie, rather [fol. 30 b.] then that I can think anye idle symbol tolerable in just orthographie.

OF THE ACCENTES OF OUR TONGUE.
Cap. 9.

1. Seing that we fynd not onelie the south and north to differ more in accent then symbol, but alsoe one word with a sundrie accent to have a diverse signification, I commend this to him quho hes auctoritie, to command al printeres and wryteres to noat the accented syllab in everie word with noe lesse diligence then we see the grecianes to noat their's.

2. Cicero, in his buik de oratore ad Brutum, makes it a natural harmonie that everie word [fol. 31 a.] pronunced be the mouth of man have one acute syllab, and that never farther from the end then the third syllab, quhilk the grammareanes cales to the same end the antepenult. Quhilk observation of so noble a wit is most true in tongues quhilk he understud, the greek and latin. But if Cicero had understud our tongue, he sould have hard the accent in the fourth syllab from the end; as in mátrimonie, pátrimonie, vádimonie, intóllerable, intélligences, and whole garrisones of lyke liverie. This anie eare may [fol. 31 b.] if he accent the antepenult matrímonie, or the penult matrimonie, or the last as matrimoníe.

3. Then to the purpose we have the same accentes quhilk the latin and the greek hath, acute, circumflex, and grave.

4. The acute raiseth the syllab quheron it sittes; as profésse, prófit, ímpudent.

5. It may possesse the last syllab : as supprést, preténce, sincére ; The penult : as súbject, cándle, cráftie[1]; The antepenult : as diffícultie, mínister, fínallie ; And the fourth also from the end, as is said sect. 2 ; as spéciallie, insátiable, díligentlie. In al quhilk, if a man change the accent, he sall spill the sound of the word.

[fol. 32 a.] 6. The grave accent is never noated, but onelie under-

---
[1] MS. crástie.

stood in al syllabes quherin the acute and circumflex is not. Onlie, for difference, sum wordes ar marked with it, thus `, leaning contrarie to the acute.

7. The circumflex accent both liftes and felles the syllab that it possesseth, and combynes *the* markes of the other tuae, thus ^. Of this we, as the latines, hes almost no use. But the south hath great use of it, and in that their dialect differes more from our's then in other soundes or symboles.

8. The use of the accent wil be of good importance for the right pronu*n*ciation of our tongue, quhilk now we doe forte, non arte, and conforming of the dialectes, qu*hi*lk, as I have said, differes most in this.

[fol. 3: b.] OF THE APOSTROPHUS AND HYPHEN.

CAP. 10.

1. The learned printeres uses to symboliz apostrophus and hyphen as wel as a, b, c.

2. Apostrophus is the ejecting of a letter or a syllab out of one word or out betuene tuae, and is alwayes marked above the lyne, as it wer a *comma*, thus '.

3. Out of one word the apostrophus is most usual in poesie; as ps. 73, v. 3, for quhen I sau such foolish men, I grug'd, and did disdain; and v. 19, They are destroy'd, dispatch'd, consum'd.

4. Betuene tuae wordes we abate either from the end of the former or the beginni*n*g of the later.

5. We abate from the end of the former quhen it endes in a voual [fol. 33 a.] and the next beginnes at a voual; As, th' ingrate; th' one parte; I s' it, for I see it.

6. In abating from the word following, we, in the north, use a mervelouse libertie; As, he's a wyse man, for he is a wyse man; I'l meet with him, for I wil meet with him; a ship 'l of fooles, for a ship ful of fooles; and this we use in our *common* language. And qu*hi*lk is stranger, we manie tymes cut of the end of the word; as, he 's tell the, for he sal tell the.

7. This for apostrophus. Hyphen is, as it wer, a band uniting whol wordes joined in composition; as, a hand-maed, a heard-man, tongue- [fol. 33 b.] tyed, out-rage, foer-warned, mis-reported, fals-deemed.

OF THE CONGRUITIE
OF OUR BRITAN
TONGUE.

LIB. 2.

OF THE PERSON.
Cap. 1.

[fol. 35 a.]

1. Al wordes q*uh*ilk we use to expresse our mynde are personal or impersonal.

2. A personal word is q*uh*ilk admittes diversitie of person.

3. Person is the face of a word, quhilk in diverse formes of speach it diverselie putes on; as, I, Peter, say that thou art the son of God. Thou, peter, sayes that I am the son of God. Peter said that I am the son of God.

4. Quherupon person is first, second, and third.

5. The first person is of him that speakes; as, I wryte.

[fol. 35 b.] 6. The second person is of him that is spoaken to; as, thou wrytes.

7. The third person is of him that is spoaken of; as, Peter wrytes.

OF NU*M*BER.
Cap. 2.

1. Number is distinction of person be one and moe; and soe is singular and plural.

2. The singular speakes of one; as, a hand, a tree, a sheep, a horse, a man.

3. The plural speakes of moe then one; as, handes, trees, sheep, horses, men, tuo, three, foure, or moe, or how manie soever.

4. This difference is commonlie noted with es at the end [fol. 36 a.] of the word singular; as, a house, houses; a windoe, windoes; a doore, tuo doores.

5. Sum tymes it is noated be changing a letter; as, a man, men; a woman, wemen; a goose, geese.

6. Sum tyme be changing noe thing; as, a sheep, a thousand sheep; a horse, an hundred horse; a noute, ten noute.

OF THE DETERMINATION OF THE PERSON.
Cap. 3.

1. A personal word is a noun or a verb. A noun is a word of one person with gender and case; as, I is onelie of the first person; [fol. 36 b.] thou is onelie of the second; and al other nounes are onelie the third person; as, Ihon, Thomas, head, hand, stone, blok, except they be joined with I or thou.

2. The person of a noun singular is determined or undetermined.

3. The determined person is noated with the, and it is determined either be an other substantive; as, the king of Britan; or be an adjective; as, the best king in Europ; or be a relative; as, God preserve the king quhom he hath geven us.

4. The undetermined noun is noated with an befoer a voual; as, an ald man sould be wyse; and with a befoer a consonant; as, a father sould command his son.

OF THE GENDER OF A NOUN.
Cap. 4.

1. Gender is the affection of a [fol. 37 a.] noun for distinction of sex.

2. Sex is a distinction of a noun be male and female, and these are distinguished the one from the other, or both from thinges without sex.

3. The one is distinguished from the other be he and she.

4. He is the noat of the male; as, he is a gud judge; he is a wyse man; he is a speedie horse; he is a crouse cock; he is a fat wether.

5. She is the noat of the femal sex; as, she is a chast matron; she is a stud meer; she is a fat hen; she is a milk cowe.

6. Nounes that want sex are noated with it; as, It is a tale tree; it is a sueet aple; it is a hard flint; [fol. 37 b.] it is a faer day; it is a foul way.

7. In the plural number they are not distinguished; As, they are honest men; They are vertueouse ladies; They are highe montanes.

OF THE CASE OF THE NOUN.
Cap. 5.

1. Case is an affection of a noun for distinction of person; As, the corner stone fel on me; stone is the nominative case. The corner of

a stone hurt me; stone is the genitive case. quhat can you doe to a stone; stone is the dative case. he brak the stone; it is the accusative case. Quhy standes thou, stone? it is the vocative. and he hurt me with a stone; it is the ablative case.

2. This difference we declyne, [fol. 38 a.] not as doth the latines and greekes, be terminationes, but with noates, after the maner of the hebrues, quhilk they cal particles.

3. The nominative hath no other noat but the particle of determination; As, the peple is a beast with manie heades; a horse serves man to manie uses; men in auctoritie sould be lanternes of light.

4. Our genitive is alwayes joyned with an-other noun, and is noated with of or s.

5. With of, it followes the noun quhar-with it is joined; as, the house of a good man is wel governed.

6. With s it preceedes the word quherof it is governed, and s is divyded from it with an apostrophus; As, a gud man's house is wel governed.

[fol. 38 b.] 7. This s sum haldes to be a segment of his, and therfoer now almost al wrytes his for it, as if it wer a corruption. But it is not a segment of his; 1. because his is the masculin gender, and this may be fœminin; As, a mother's love is tender; 2. because his is onelie singular, and this may be plural; as, al men's vertues are not knawen.

8. The dative is noated with to, and for; as, geve libertie evin to the best youth and it wil luxuriat. Al men doeth for them-selves; few for a frende.

9. The accusative hath noe other noat then the nominative; as, the head governes the bodie.

10. The vocative is the person to quhom the speach is directed; as, quhence cumes thou, æneas?

[fol. 39 a.] 11. The ablative is noated with prepositiones in, with, be, and sik lyke; as, be god al thinges wer made; God with his word his warkes began; In my father's house are manie mansiones.

OF THE DEGREES OF COMPARISON.
Cap. 6.

1. Al nounes that wil join with a substantive ar called adjectives; as, gud, high, hard, sueet, sour.

2. These, and al that wil admit mare and mast, are compared be degrees; as, sueet, more sueet, most sueet.

3. Of comparison ther be thre degrees: the positive, comparative, and superlative, if the first may be called a degre.

4. The positive is the first [fol. 39 b.] position of the noun; as, soft, hard; quhyte, blak; hoat, cald.

5. The comparative excedes the positive be mare, and is formed of the positive be adding er; as, softer, harder; quhiter, blaker; hoater, calder.

6. The superlative excedes the positive be most, and is formed of the positive be adding est; as, softest, hardest; quhytest, blakest; hoatest, caldest.

OF THE VERB'S PERSON AND NUMBER.
Cap. 7.

1. This for the noun. The verb is a word of al persones declyned with mood and tyme; as, I wryte, thou writes, he wrytes.

2. We declyne not the persones and numberes of the verb, as doth the latine, but noat them be the person of the noun.

3. They are noated with I, thou, and [fol. 40 a.] he in the singular number; we, ye, and they in the plural.

4. The number is noated with I and we; thou and ye; he and they.

OF THE MOOD OF THE VERB.
Cap. 8.

1. The mood is an affection of the verb serving the varietie of utterance.

2. We utter the being of thinges or our awn wil.

3. The being of thinges is uttered be inquyring or avouing.

4. We inquyre of that we wald knaw; as, Made God man without synne? and in this the supposit of the verb followes the verb.

5. We avoue that quhilk we knaw; as, God made man without sinne; and in this the supposit precedes the verb.

6. We utter our wil be verbes signifying the form of our wil, [fol. 40 b.] or postposing the supposit.

7. We wish be wald god, god grant, and god nor; as, wald god I knew the secretes of nature.

8. We permit the will of otheres be letting; as, let God aryse; let everie man have his awn wyfe.

9. We bid our inferioures, and pray our superioures, be postponing the supposit to the verb; As, goe ye and teach al nationes; Here me, my God.

OF THE TYME OF THE VERB.
Cap. 9.

1. Tyme is an affection of the verb noating the differences of tyme, and is either present, past, or to cumm.

2. Tyme present is that quhilk now is; as, I wryte, or am wryting.

3. Tyme past is that quhilk was, and it is passing befoer, past els, or past befoer.

4. Tyme passing befoer, quhilk we cal imperfectlie past, is of a thing [fol. 41 a.] that was doeing but not done; as, at four hoores I was wryting; Quhen you spak to me I was wryting, or did wryte, as lillie expoundes it.

5. Tyme past els is of a thing now past, quhilk we cal perfectlie past; As, I have written.

6. Tyme past befoer is of a thing befoer done and ended; as, at four hoores, or quhen you spak to me, I had written.

7. Tyme to cum is of that quhilk is not yet begun; As, at four houres I wil wryte.

OF THE POWER OF THE VERB.
Cap. 10.

1. A verb signifies being or doeing. Of being ther is onelie one, I am, and is thus varyed.

OF THE CONGRUITIE

2. In the present tyme, I am, thou art, he is ; we are, ye are, they are.

[fol. 41 b.] 3. In tyme passing befoer, I was, thou was, he was ; we wer, ye wer, they wer.

4. In tyme past els, I have bene, thou hes bene, he hes bene ; we have bene, ye have bene, they have bene.

5. In tyme past befoer, I had bene, thou had bene, he had bene ; we had bene, ye had bene, they had bene.

6. In tyme to cum, I wil be, thou wilt be, he wil be ; we wil be, ye wil be, they wil be.

7. Verbes of doing are actives or passives.

8. The active verb adheres to the person of the agent; As, Christ hath conquered hel and death.

9. The passive verb adheres to the person of the patient; As, hel and death are conquered be Christ.

10. These our idiom conjugates onelie in tuo tymes, the tyme [fol. 42 a.] present and tym past ; as, I wryte, I wrote ; I speak, I spak ; I here, I hard ; I se, I saw ; I fele, I felt.

11. The other differences of tyme ar expressed be the notes of the verb of being, or be the verb of being it-self, and a participle ; As, I was wryting ; I have written ; I had written ; I wil wryte.

OF THE ADVERB.
Cap. 11.

1. A word impersonal is qu*hi*lk in al formes of speach keepes one face, and this is adverb or conjunction.

2. An adverb is a word adhering mast commonlie with a verb with one face in al moodes, tymes, numberes and persones ; As, I leve [fol. 42 b.] hardlie, thou leves hardlie ; I did leve hardlie ; I have leved hardlie ; I had leved hardlie ; I wil leave hardlie ; leve he hardlie ; god forbid he leve hardlie, *etc.*

3. Our men confoundes adverbes of place, qu*hi*lk the south distinguishes as wel as the latin, and therfoer let us not shame to learne.

4. They use quher, heer, ther, for the place in qu*hi*lk ; quhence, hence, thence, for the place from quhilk ; quhither, hither, thither,

for the place to q*uhi*lk ; As, quher dwel you ? quhence cum you ? quhither goe you ?

5. They also distinguish wel in, into, and unto : in, they use with the place quher ; into, with the thing quhither ; and unto, for how far ; As, our father, q*uhi*lk art in heavin, [fol. 43 a.] admit us into heavin, and lift us from the earth unto heavin.

6. Heer, becaus sum nounes incurre into adverbes, let us alsoe noat their differences.

7. First no and not. Noe is a noun, nullus in latin, and in our tongue alwayes precedes the substantive quhilk it nulleth ; as, noe man, noe angle, noe god.

8. Not is an adverb; non in latin, and in our tong followes the verb that it nulleth ; As, heer not, grant not ; I heer not, I grant not ; I wil not heer, I wil not grant.

9. Ane, in our idiom, and an. ane is a noun of number, in latin unus ; an a particule of determination preceding a voual, as we have said cap. 3, sect. 4.

[fol. 43 b.] 10. Thee and the. Thee is the accusative of thou ; As, thou loves God, and God loves thee. the is the determined no[a]t of a noun, of q*uhi*lk we spak cap. 3, sect. 3.

OF THE CONJUNCTION.
Cap. 12.

1. Conjunction is a word impersonal serving to cople diverse senses. And of it ther be tuoe sortes, the one enunciative, and the other ratiocinative.

2. The conjunction enunciative coples the partes of a period, and are copulative, as and ; Connexive, as if ; Disjunctive, as or ; or discretive, as howbeit.

3. The ratiocinative coples the partes of a ratiocination, and it either inferres the conclusion or the reason.

4. Therfoer inferres the conclusion ; [fol. 44 a.] As, Noe man can keep the law in thought, word, and deed : And therfoer noe man befoer the judg of the hart, word, and deed, can be justifyed be the law.

5. Because inferres the reason; As, I wil spew the out, because thou art nether hoat nor cald.

OF DISTINCTIONES.

Cap. 13.

1. A distinction is quherbe sentences are distinguished in wryting and reading. And this is perfect or imperfect.

2. A perfect distinction closes a perfect sense, and is marked with a round punct, thus . or a tailed punct, [fol. 44 b.] thus ?

3. The round punct concludes an assertion; as, If Abraham was justifyed be workes: he had quherof to glorie.

4. The tailed punct concludes an interrogation; As, sal we, quha are dead to synn, leve to it?

5. The imperfect distinction divydes the partes of a period, and is marked with tuoe punctes, the one under the other, thus : and is red with half the pause of a perfect punct; As, Al have synned; and fallen from the glorie of god : but are justifyed frelie be his grace.

6. The comma divydes the least partes of the period, and is pronunced in reading with a short sob.

7. The parenthesis divydes [fol. 45 a.] in the period a sentence interlaced on sum occurrentes quhilk coheres be noe syntax with that quhilk preceedes and followes; As, for exemple of beath, and to conclud this treatesse :

> Bless, guyd, advance, preserve, prolong Lord (if thy pleasur be)
> Our king, *and* Queen ; and keep their seed thy name to magnifie.

NOTES.

The foregoing Tract is one of great interest, not only on account of its intrinsic merit, but also for the racy style of writing adopted by its author. We find him continually garnishing his language with such idiomatic and colloquial expressions as the following :—" Quhae's sillie braine will reach no farther then the compas of their cap" (page 2); and again, " but wil not presume to judge farther then the compasse of my awn cap" (p. 20). He observes of the printers and writers of his age that they care " for noe more arte then may win the pennie" (p. 2), and on the same page he says, " quhiles I stack in this claye," which appears to be equivalent to our term " stuck in the mud." At p. 3 he says, " and it wer but a clod;" at p. 14, " nether daer I, with al the oares of reason, row against so strang a tyde;" and again, on p. 18, we find reason under another aspect, thus, " noe man I trow can denye that ever suked the paepes of reason."

It seems that the expression, *Queen's English*, is by no means of modern date, as we have it as the *king's language* at p. 2.

Hume laments, in his Dedication, the uncertainty of the orthography prevailing at the time he writes, and yet we find him spelling words several different ways, even within the compass of a single sentence, without being able to lay the blame upon the printers; thus we find him writing ju*d*gement on p. 11, ju*d*ge p. 8, and ju*d*g p. 33, but juge p. 18; and there are numberless other instances that it would be tedious to enumerate. Again, the author uses a mixture of Scotch and English, so we have sometimes ane and sometimes one; nae on page 1 and noe on p. 2; mast and most on the same page (p. 30); and two is spelt in three different ways, tuae, tuo, and tuoe.

Our author's stay in England appears to have drawn his attention to the differences between the two languages of Scotland and England, which he distinguishes as North and South. He certainly shows, in some instances, the greater correctness of the Scotch with regard to the spelling of words derived from the Latin ; as, retine instead of retain, corage instead of courage, etc. (p. 20), in which words the redundant letters that the Southerners have introduced are thrown out. He is, however, by no means partial, and gives us praise when he thinks we deserve it.

Page 9. The arguments in favour of the sound given by the English Universities to the Latin *i* are curious : it is stated to have its value in the Greek ει ; but the author seems to have been in error as to the English sounding mihi and tibi alike, or our pronunciation must have changed since his time.

P. 10. The author speaks of the letter *y* as being used by the South for the sound now symbolized by *i* with a final *e* following the succeeding consonant, as *uill* with an *i*, and *wile* with a *y* in place of the *i* and final *e*; thus in the same way he spells write, *wryt*.

P. 11 (7). He gives food, good, blood, as examples of the same sound, thus inferring that the English pronounced the two latter so as to rhyme with food.

P. 11 (8). He objects to the use of *w* for *u* in the diphthongal sound of *ou*, and therefore spells *how, now*, etc., *hou, nou*.

P. 13 (12). The author here recommends the distinction both of sound and symbol of *j* and *v* as consonants, and *i* and *u* as vowels, and proposes that we should call *j jod* or *je*, and *v vau* or *ve*, and not single *u*, "as now they doe" (p. 16), and *w* he would call *wau* or *we*, and moreover he places them in his alphabet on the same page. If this proposal was originally his own, it is curious that the name *ve* should have been adopted, though not the *we* for *w*. Ben Jonson points out the double power of *i* and *v* as both consonant and vowel, but he does not attempt to make them into separate letters as Hume does.

P. 15 (12). He gives as an anomaly of the South that while the *d* is inserted before *g* in hedge, bridge, etc., it is omitted in age, suage, etc. He does not see that the short vowel requires a double consonant to prevent it from being pronounced long.

P. 21 (6). He disputes the possibility of a final *e*, separated from a preceding vowel by a consonant, having any effect whatever in altering the sound of the preceding vowel, and recommends the use of a diphthong to express the sound required; as, hoep for hope, fier for fire, bied for bide, befoer for before, maed for made, etc. He uniformly throughout follows this rule.

P. 23 (7). He puts down outrage as an instance of two distinct words joined by a hyphen, which is the derivation given by Ash in his dictionary, in strange obliviousness of the French word *outrage*.

P. 27 (1, 6). *T* is omitted after *s* in the second person singular of the verb, and so no distinction is made between the second and the third persons; thus, thou wrytes, and at p. 32 thou was, and thou hes.

P. 29 (7). The supposition that the apostrophe's as a mark of the possessive case is a segment of his, a question which has been lately revived, is here denied.

P. 34. In this last chapter on Punctuation, which the author styles "of Distinctiones," no mention whatever is made of the "semicolon," though it occurs frequently in the MS., as, for instance, p. 30, cap. 6. This stop, according to Herbert, was first used by Richard Grafton in *The Byble* printed in 1537 : it occurs in the Dedication. Henry Denham, an English printer who flourished towards the close of the sixteenth century, was the first to use it with propriety.

P. 34 (6). The explanation of the mode of pronouncing the comma "with a short *sob*" is odd.[1]

The author continually uses a singular verb to a plural noun; for instance, "of this we, as the latines, hes almost no use" (p. 23), though on p. 20 he writes, "in our tongue we have sum particles."

With regard to the Manuscript, there are two corrections in it worth noting. At p. 10 (6), in the phrase, "the auctours *whole* drift," the word had been originally written *hael*, but is marked through, and *whole* substituted for it in the same handwriting. At p. 21 (4), the word *frensh* has been inserted before *exemples*, but has been afterwards struck through.

The numbering is wrong in three places, but it has not been corrected. At p. 8 there are no sections 12 and 13, at pp. 17, 19, there are two cap. 7, and at p. 19 there are two sections 4.

[1] It will be here as well to mention that as the punctuation in the MS. is extremely unsystematic, it has been dispensed with whenever the meaning was confused by it.

GLOSSARIAL INDEX.

[The words in the present Tract that really required to be glossed are but few; I have, however, inserted in the following list most of the variations from ordinary modern usage, in order that it may serve as an Index.]

Af = of, p. 9. Af = off, p. 12.
Ald = old, pp. 3, 22, 28.
Amangs = amongst, p. 18.
Ane = a, one.
Angle = angel, p. 33.
Auctoritie = authority, pp. 22, 29.
Aun = own, pp. 2, 3, 7, 8, 11, 16.
Awn = own, pp. 11, 16, 18, 20, 30, 31.
Awn = proper, pp. 9, 11, 13, 15.
Awne = proper, p. 14.
Awne = own, p. 10.
Baeth = both, pp. 8, 34.
Bathe = both, p. 18.
Be = by.
Britan = British.
Cald = cold, pp. 30, 34; caldest, p. 30.
Cales = calls, pp. 10, 22.
Chirt = a squirt, or a squeeze through the teeth, pp. 13, 14. See Ruddiman's Glossary to G. Douglas (*chirtand*).
Cold = could, p. 20.
Coples = couples, p. 33.
Corage = courage, p. 20.
Crouse = brisk, p. 28.
Cum = come, pp. 11, 31; cumes = comes, pp. 21, 29.
Devore = devour, p. 20.
Devote = devout, p. 20.
Distinctiones = punctuation, p. 34.
Doon = done, p. 21.
Doting = giving, p. 3.

Earand = errand, p. 8.
Evin = even, p. 29.
Faer = fair, p. 28.
Falt = fault, pp. 15, 20.
Fand = found, p. 1.
Fele = feel, p. 32.
Felles = lowers, p. 23.
Finnes = fineness, p. 2.
Fontan = fountain, p. 11.
Foran = foreign, p. 20.
Frelie = freely, p. 34.
Geve = give, pp. 7, 8, 9, 12, 28, 29.
Gif = if, p. 21.
Glim = glimpse, p. 2.
Gud = good, pp. 2, 18, 21, 28, 30.
Hael = hail, p. 10.
Hald = hold, p. 14; haldes, p. 29.
Hame = home, p. 2.
Hard = heard, pp. 2, 3, 13, 14, 22, 32.
Hart = heart, p. 33.
Heal = whole, p. 10.
Heer = hear, p. 33.
Here = hear, pp. 31, 32.
Hes = has, pp. 3, 14, 15, 20, 22, 32.
Hes = hast, p. 32.
Hes = have, pp. 20, 23.
Hoat = hot, pp. 18, 30, 34; hoater, p. 30.
Hoores = hours, p. 31.
Ida, Scotland or Edinburgh, p. 2.
Incurre, v. = to run into. Lat. *incurro*, pp. 20, 33.

Ken = know, p. 22.
Kep, v. = to intercept, p. 14.
Kepping = receiving in the act of falling, p. 12. *Jamieson.*
Knau = know, p. 2.
Knaulege = knowledge, pp. 3, 10; knawlege, pp. 11, 22.
Knaw = know, pp. 7, 31; knawe, p. 21; knawen = known, p. 29.
Laggared = loitered or rested, p. 2.
Lang = long, pp. 9, 14.
Leave = live, p. 32.
Leve = live, pp. 32, 34.
Leving = living, p. 11.
Louse = loose, p. 9.
Lykwayes = likewise, p. 19.
Maer = more, pp. 2, 10.
Maest = most, pp. 1, 2, 16.
Man = must, p. 8.
Mare = more, p. 30.
Mast = most, pp. 30, 32.
Meer = mare, p. 28.
Middes = middle, p. 16.
Mikle = much, pp. 13, 19, 20.
Mint = aim, pressure, p. 18.
Minted = attempted, p. 15.
Moat, probably *moot*, discussion, chat, etc., p. 2. A.S. *mót.* Perhaps a miswriting for meat.
Moe = more, pp. 16, 19, 22, 27.
Moien = means for attaining an end, p. 2. *Jamieson.* Fr. *moyen.*
Mont = mount, p. 24.
Montan = mountain, pp. 3, 11, 28.
Mynt = aim, pp. 12, 17.
Nae = no, pp. 1, 8.
Nane = none, p. 13.
Noat, v. = note, pp. 20, 22, 27, 28, 29, 30, 31, 33.
Noat = note, pp. 7, 13, 28, 29; noate, p. 28; noates = notes, p. 29.
Nor = than, p. 3.
Nor, God nor, p. 31. This most probably means God comfort or nourish us, connected with *no-rice*, a nurse, and *norie*, a foster-child. There is also a substantive *nore* in Chaucer, meaning comfort. *Norne* is to entreat, ask (see *Alliterative Poems* Glossary), and may have something to do with this expression, but it is hardly so probable as the above.
Noute = black cattle, p. 27; connected with *neat*, as in neat-cattle, neat-herd.
Nulleth = negatives, p. 33.
Nurice = nurse, p. 20.
Of = off, p. 23.
Ones, at ones = at once, p. 18.
Paen = trouble, p. 2.
Paert = part, p. 10.
Peple = people, pp. 20, 29.
Phason = pheasant (?), p. 13.
Pover = poor, p. 3.
Punct = stop, p. 34.
Qu. At p. 18 the author gives his reasons for making use of the guttural *qu* in the place of the labial *w.* The following are the words in which it is thus used:—
Quha = who, pp. 2, 3, 34.
Quhae = who, pp. 1, 10; quhae's = whose, p. 2.
Quhaer = where, p. 2.
Quhar = where, p. 29.
Quharein = wherein, p. 14.
Quharof = whereof, p. 16.
Quhat = what, pp. 2, 8, 15, 17, 18, 29.
Quhatever = whatever, p. 19.
Quhen = when, pp. 2, 9, 11, 17, 23, 31.
Quhence = whence, pp. 29, 33.
Quher = where, pp. 2, 14, 20, 33.
Quheras = whereas, p. 15.
Quherat = whereat, p. 18.
Quherbe = whereby, pp. 12, 34.
Quherfoer, quherforr = wherefore, pp. 7, 8, 10, 15.

40 GLOSSARIAL INDEX.

Quherin = wherein, pp. 20, 23.
Quherof = whereof, pp. 29, 34.
Quheron = whereon, p. 22.
Quherupon=whereupon, pp. 8, 27.
Quherwith = wherewith, p. 2.
Quhil, quhiles = while, p. 2.
Quhilk = which.
Quhither = whether, pp. 11, 17, 19, 20, 33.
Quho = who, pp. 12, 14, 15, 19, 22.
Quhom = whom.
Quhy = why, pp. 21, 29.
Quhyte = white, p. 30; quhiter, p. 30; quhytest, p. 30.
Quod = quoth, p. 18.
Rease = rose, p. 18.
Red = read, p. 34.
Regne = reign, p. 20.
Retine = retain, p. 20.
Ryseth = ariseth, p. 9.
Sa = so, p. 21; sae = so, p. 17.
Sal = shall, pp. 9, 11, 23, 34.
Sall = shall, pp. 8, 22.
Shaued = showed, p. 7.
Shour = shower, p. 10.
Sib = related, p. 21.
Sik = such, pp. 1, 2, 8, 9, 11, 17, 29.
Sillie = wretched, poor, p. 2.
Skaiographie = bad spelling, p. 2. From σκαιος, left, left-handed, awkward, crooked, opposed to ὀρθὸς. Lat. scœvus.
Sould = should, pp. 7, 9, 11, 12, 13, 17, 18, 19, 22, 28, 29.
Spering = inquiring, p. 18.
Spil = destroy, spoil (?), p. 13; spill, p. 22.
Spilt = corrupted, spoilt (?), p. 2.
Stack = stuck, p. 2.
Stean = stone, p. 8.
Stiddie = anvil, pp. 12, 17.
"But he is a servant as well of Apollo as Vulcan, turning his *stiddy* into a study."—*Fuller's Worthies*, ed. 1840, vol. 2, p. 295.
Strang = strong, p. 14.
Sum = some, pp. 8, 9, 10, 20, 21, 23, 34.
Supposit = subject, p. 31.
Syllab = syllable, pp. 14, 15, 16, 17, 18, 21, 22; syllabes, p. 8, 23. Ben Jonson spells this word *syllabe* in his English Grammar.
Syne = since, p. 1.
Tal = tale, p. 9.
Tal = tail, p. 9.
Tale = tall, p. 28.
Trow = believe, pp. 14, 18, 21.
Tuae = two, pp. 1, 8, 9, 10, 22, 23.
Tuelfe = twelve, p. 3.
Tuich = touch, pp. 7, 13, 15, 17; tuiches, p. 11.
Tuiched = touched, pp. 3, 18.
Tuich stone = touchstone, p. 20.
Tyme passing befoer = imperfect tense, pp. 31, 32.
Tyme past befoer = pluperfect tense, pp. 31, 32.
Tyme past els = perfect tense, pp. 31, 32.
Vadimonie = recognisance, p. 22. Lat. *Vadimonium*.
Voce = voice, p. 20.
Waet = know, p. 14.
Wait = know, p. 11.
Wald = would, pp. 1, 2, 9, 10, 13, 15, 16, 21, 30, 31.
Warkes = works, p. 29.
Weer = war, p. 3.
Were = war, p. 20.
Whither = whether, p. 2. The author in this place uses the letter *w* instead of *qu*, although at p. 18 he is so strenuous against its use.
Wrang = wrong, pp. 2, 9, 11.
Ye = yea, p. 14.
Yeld = yield, p. 21.

The manufacturer's authorised representative in the EU for product
safety is Oxford University Press España S.A. of El Parque Empresarial
San Fernando de Henares, Avenida de Castilla, 2 - 28830 Madrid
(www.oup.es/en or product.safety@oup.com). OUP España S.A. also acts
as importer into Spain of products made by the manufacturer.
Printed and bound by CPI Group (UK) Ltd, Croydon, CR0 4YY

20/03/2026

02075338-0001